Introduction

When people are asked what it is that they would like to have more of, one common answer is time. It seems like schedules are so full with family, work, housework, shopping, cooking—the list goes on and on. Quilters are no exception—they are busy but want the luxury of time to work on their craft.

We've created this pattern book with busy quilters in mind. The patterns in this book are all ones that can be made in a day or less. With a little preplanning and prep, a leisurely day can be spent creating a quilt top—whether it's on a quilting retreat, a rainy day or just some time set aside.

Pull up a chair, browse through this book and make a plan for your next bit of free time.

Table of Contents

3 Wish Making

6 Sandy Shores

11 Color Me Happy

13 Square Dance

17 Slice of My Heart

20 Blueberry Cobbler

25 Simply Charming

28 Batik Waffles

31 Stairway to Heaven

34 Crisscross Throw

37 Sidestep

40 Summer Breeze

44 Wash Day

General Information

47 Quilting Basics

48 Special Thanks

48 Supplies

Inspiration

"I have long been a fan of the Ribbon Star block, and I love how the wide stripes echo the shapes of the star points." —Andy Knowlton

Wish Making

Bold, wide stripes make this a quick quilt to piece. Use red, white and blue prints for a quick summertime quilt or reds and greens for a holiday version!

Design by Andy Knowlton of A Bright Corner
Quilted by Kaitlyn Howell of Knot and Thread Design

Skill Level
Confident Beginner

Finished Sizes
Quilt Size: 51" x 66"
Block Size: 12" x 12"
Number of Blocks: 5

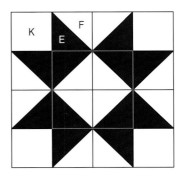

Ribbon Star
12" x 12" Finished Block
Make 5

Materials
- 2¼ yards white solid
- 1 yard navy blue tonal*
- ⅜ yard each dark red, pink, dark blue, aqua and red plaid prints*
- 3½ yards backing
- 61" x 76" batting
- Thread
- Basic sewing tools and supplies

Fabrics from Berry Basket by April Rosenthal for Moda Fabrics used to make sample.

Project Notes
Read all instructions before beginning this project.

Stitch right sides together using a ¼" seam allowance unless otherwise specified.

Materials and cutting lists assume 40" of usable fabric width for yardage.

Arrows indicate directions to press seams.

WOF – width of fabric
HST – half-square triangle ◻
QST – quarter-square triangle ⊠

Cutting

From length of white solid cut:
- 2 (3½" x 51½") M strips
- 4 (3½" x 37½") G strips
- 4 (3½" x 29½") H strips
- 4 (3½" x 20") I strips
- 4 (3½" x 10½") J strips
- 8 (8") F squares
- 36 (3½") K squares
- 2 (2½" x 12½") L strips

From navy blue tonal cut:
- 8 (8") E squares
- 7 (2½" x WOF) binding strips

From dark red print cut:
- 1 (6½" x 37½") A strip

From pink print cut:
- 1 (6½" x 29½") B strip
- 1 (6½" x 10½") C strip

From dark blue print cut:
- 1 (6½" x 29½") B strip
- 1 (6½" x 10½") C strip

From aqua print cut:
- 1 (6½" x 37½") A strip

From red plaid print cut:
- 2 (6½" x 20") D strips

Completing the Blocks

1. Refer to Eight-at-a-Time Half-Square Triangles to make eight E-F units using one each E and F square (Figure 1). Trim the units to 3½" x 3½". Make 64.

E-F Unit
Make 64

Figure 1

2. Arrange 12 E-F units and four K squares in four rows; sew into rows then sew the rows together to complete one Ribbon Star block (Figure 2). Make five. **Note:** *There will be four E-F units left that will not be used.*

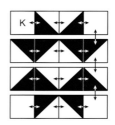
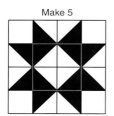

Make 5

Figure 2

Completing the Quilt

1. Refer to Sew & Flip Corners on page 12 to add two adjacent corner triangles on one end of an A strip using two K squares to complete one A-K strip (Figure 3). Make two.

A-K Strip
Make 2

A

K

Figure 3

2. Repeat step 1 to add two adjacent corner triangles on one end of the B, C and D strips using K squares to complete two each B-K, C-K and D-K strips.

3. Sew a G strip to both long sides of an A-K strip to complete one A-G-K strip (Figure 4). Make two.

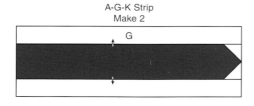

A-G-K Strip
Make 2

G

Figure 4

EIGHT-AT-A-TIME HALF-SQUARE TRIANGLES

Half-square triangles (HSTs) are a basic unit of quilting used in many blocks or on their own. This construction method will yield eight HST units.

1. Refer to the pattern for size to cut squares. The standard formula is to add 1" to the finished size of the square then multiply by 2. Cut two squares from different colors this size. For example, for a 3" finished HST unit, cut 8" squares (3" + 1" = 4"; 4" x 2 = 8").

2. Draw two diagonal lines from corner to corner on the wrong side of the lightest color square. Layer the squares right sides together. Stitch ¼" on either side of both drawn lines (Figure A).

Figure A

3. Cut the sewn squares in half horizontally and vertically, making four squares. Then cut each square apart on the drawn line, leaving a ¼" seam allowance and making eight HST units referring to Figure B. Trim each HST unit to the desired size (3½" in this example).

Figure B

4. Open the HST units and press seam allowances toward the darker fabric making eight HST units (Figure C). ●

Figure C

4. Repeat step 3 to make the following:

- two B-H-K strips using two B-K strips and four H strips
- two C-J-K strips using two C-K strips and four J strips
- two D-I-K strips using two D-K strips and four I strips.

5. Referring to the Assembly Diagram and noting fabric orientation, arrange the Ribbon Star blocks, A-G-K strips, B-H-K strips, C-J-K strips, D-I-K strips and L and M strips in seven rows. Sew into rows then sew the rows together to complete the quilt top.

6. Layer, baste, quilt as desired and bind referring to Quilting Basics. The photographed quilt was quilted with an allover flower design. ●

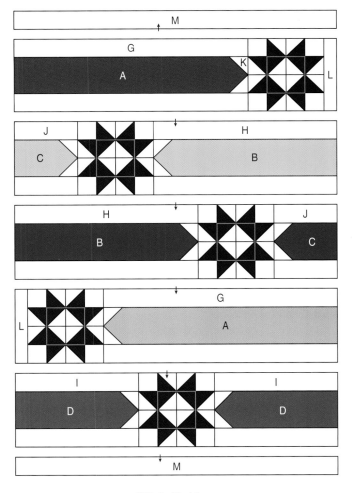

Wish Making
Assembly Diagram 51" x 66"

Sandy Shores

Create your own beach with some water- and sand-colored precut strips.

Designed & Quilted by Scott A. Flanagan

Skill Level

Beginner

Finished Sizes

Quilt Size: 56" x 68"
Block Size: 8" x 12"
Number of Blocks: 30

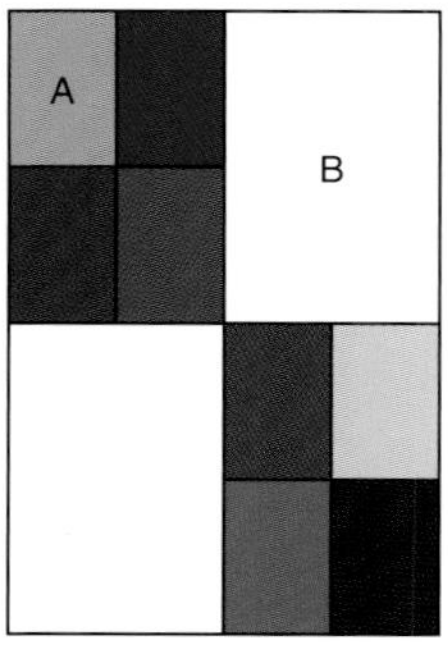

Double Four-Patch
8" x 12" Finished Block
Make 30

Materials

- 20 assorted 2½" strips
- 1¾ yards background fabric
- 1⅝ yards border/binding fabric
- 3⅝ yards backing fabric
- 64" x 76" batting*
- Thread
- Basic sewing tools and supplies

**Warm & Natural: Warm 100 batting from The Warm Company used to make sample.*

Project Notes

Read all instructions before beginning this project.

Stitch right sides together using a ¼" seam allowance unless otherwise specified.

Materials and cutting lists assume 40" of usable fabric width for yardage.

Arrows indicate directions to press seams.

WOF – width of fabric
HST – half-square triangle
QST – quarter-square triangle

Cutting

From assorted strips cut:

- 240 (2½" x 3½") A rectangles

From background fabric cut:

- 60 (4½" x 6½") B rectangles

From border/binding fabric cut:

- 7 (4½" x WOF) C/D border strips
- 7 (2½" x WOF) binding strips

Completing the Blocks

1. Lay out four A rectangles in two rows of two rectangles. Sew rectangles together in rows; join the rows to make a four-patch unit (Figure 1). Make 60.

Four-Patch Unit
Make 60

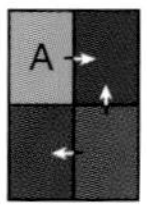

Figure 1

2. Sew a B rectangle to a four-patch unit as shown (Figure 2). Make 60.

Make 60

Figure 2

3. Refer to the Double Four-Patch block diagram and arrange two step 2 units as shown. Join the units to complete one block. Make 30.

Completing the Quilt

1. Refer to the Assembly Diagram and lay out the blocks in five rows of six blocks each.

2. Sew the blocks together in rows; join the rows to complete the quilt center. Press.

3. Sew the C/D border strips together, short ends to short ends. Referring to Determining Border Lengths, measure and cut C and D border strips and sew borders to the quilt top in alphabetical order.

4. Layer, baste, quilt as desired and bind referring to Quilting Basics. The photographed quilt was quilted with a large ocean wave design. ●

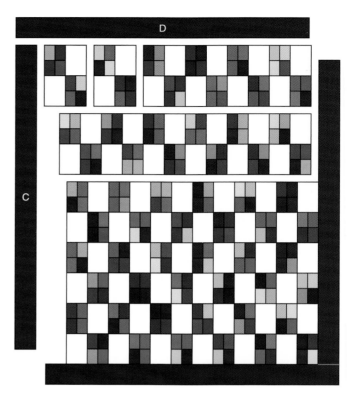

Sandy Shores
Assembly Diagram 56" x 68"

DETERMINING BORDER LENGTHS

To measure for straight, plain borders:

1. Lay the pieced quilt top on a flat surface.

2. Measure the quilt top through the center from top to bottom. Side borders will be cut to this length and sewn to opposite sides of quilt top before adding top and bottom borders.

3. Measure the quilt top through the center from side to side. Add twice the finished width of the side borders plus ½" for seams

to this measurement to determine the length to cut the top and bottom borders.

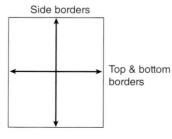

Side borders

Top & bottom borders

Measuring for Border Lengths

4. Borders can be cut along the lengthwise grain or crosswise grain of the fabric. A lengthwise cut will give you borders with no seams cut the total length needed. A crosswise cut requires that you cut the fabric width into strips to total the length of the border and then stitch them together to make the total length needed.

Note: If making mitered borders, add at least twice the border width to border lengths. ●

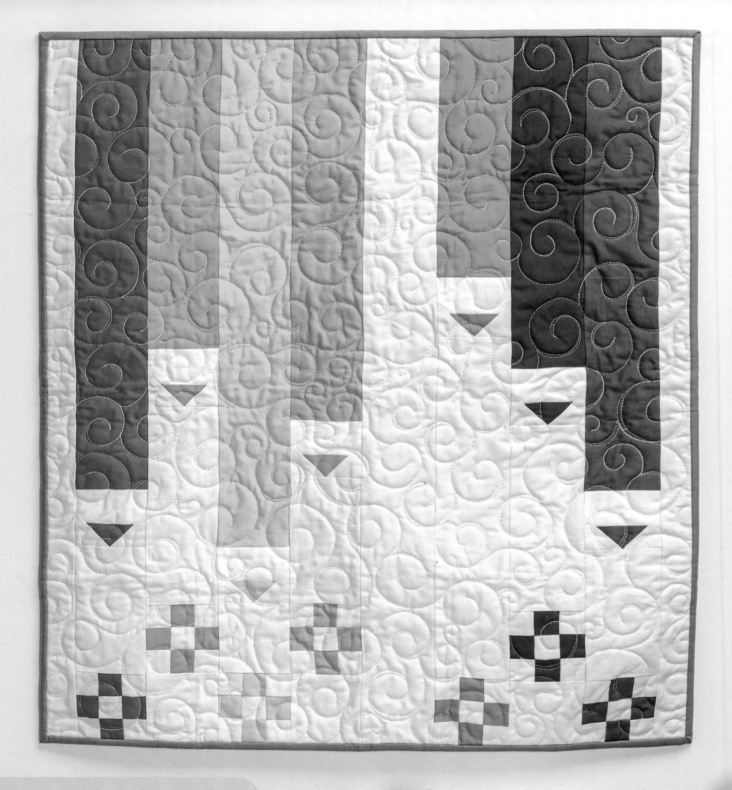

Inspiration

"This design is inspired by how particular my daughter was about arranging her crayons or colored pencils just so when she was learning to color during her toddler years." —Wendy Sheppard

Color Me Happy

Here's a colorful quilt that will bring delight to a child—or to someone who is young at heart.

Designed & Quilted by Wendy Sheppard

Skill Level

Confident Beginner

Finished Sizes

Quilt Size: 27" x 30"
Block Size: 2½" x 3" and 3" x 3"
Number of Blocks: 7 and 7

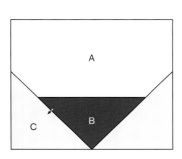

Pencil Tip
2¹⁄₂" x 3" Finished Block
Make 7

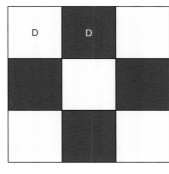

Nine-Patch
3" x 3" Finished Block
Make 7

Materials

- ⅔ yard background fabric*
- ¼ yard each red, orange, yellow, green, blue, indigo, purple and white solids*
- ⅜ yard gray solid*
- 1 yard backing fabric*
- 35" x 36" batting*
- Thread*
- Basic sewing tools and supplies

Fabrics from Bella Solids by Moda Fabrics; 50 wt. Mako thread from Aurifil; Tuscany silk batting from Hobbs Bonded Fibers used to make sample. EQ8 was used to design this quilt.

Project Notes

Read all instructions before beginning this project.

Stitch right sides together using a ¼" seam allowance unless otherwise specified.

Materials and cutting lists assume 40" of usable fabric width for yardage.

Arrows indicate directions to press seams.

WOF – width of fabric
HST – half-square triangle ▢
QST – quarter-square triangle ▣

Cutting

From background fabric cut:

- 1 (3½" x 30½") P strip
- 1 (3½" x 15") M rectangle
- 1 (3½" x 9") H rectangle
- 1 (3½" x 8") O rectangle
- 3 (3½" x 6") F rectangles
- 4 (3½") I squares
- 2 (2" x 30½") Q strips
- 14 (2") C squares
- 35 (1½") D squares

From white solid cut:

- 7 (2" x 3½") A rectangles

From each red and purple solid cut:

- 1 (3½" x 19½") E rectangle
- 1 (1½" x 3½") B rectangle
- 4 (1½") D squares

From orange solid cut:

- 1 (3½" x 13½") G rectangle
- 1 (1½" x 3½") B rectangle
- 4 (1½") D squares

From yellow solid cut:
- 1 (3½" x 22") J rectangle
- 1 (1½" x 3½") B rectangle
- 4 (1½") D squares

From green solid cut:
- 1 (3½" x 16½") K rectangle
- 1 (1½" x 3½") B rectangle
- 4 (1½") D squares

From blue solid cut:
- 1 (3½" x 10½") L rectangle
- 1 (1½" x 3½") B rectangle
- 4 (1½") D squares

From indigo solid cut:
- 1 (3½" x 14½") N rectangle
- 1 (1½" x 3½") B rectangle
- 4 (1½") D squares

From gray solid cut:
- 4 (2½" x WOF) binding strips

Completing the Blocks

1. Sew one A rectangle to one B rectangle along the long edge (Figure 1). Make seven.

2. Refer to the Pencil Tip block diagram and Sew & Flip Corners and sew two C squares to lower B corners of a step 1 unit. Make seven.

3. Referring to the Nine-Patch block diagram, arrange five background fabric D squares and four

red D squares in three rows. Join the squares in rows; join the rows to complete one block. Repeat with the remaining D squares to make seven blocks.

Completing the Quilt

1. Referring to the Assembly Diagram, arrange E–O rectangles, pencil tip blocks and Nine-Patch blocks in vertical rows as shown. Sew together the rectangles and blocks in vertical rows.

2. Join the step 1 vertical rows, P strip and Q strips as shown to complete the quilt top.

3. Layer, baste, quilt as desired and bind referring to Quilting Basics. The photographed quilt was quilted with swirls. ●

Make 7

A
↓
B

Figure 1

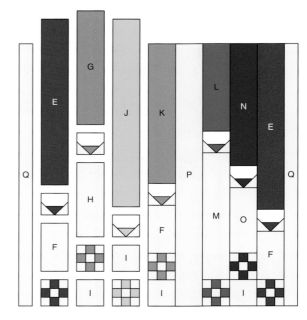

Color Me Happy
Assembly Diagram 27" x 30"

SEW & FLIP CORNERS

Use this method to add triangle corners in a quilt block.

1. Draw a diagonal line from corner to corner on the wrong side of the specified square. Place the square, right sides together, on the indicated corner of the larger piece, making sure the line is oriented in the correct direction indicated by the pattern (Figure 1).

2. Sew on the drawn line. Trim ¼" away from sewn line (Figure 2).

Figure 1

Figure 2

3. Open and press to reveal the corner triangle (Figure 3).

Figure 3

4. If desired, square up the finished unit to the required unfinished size. ●

Square Dance

Do-si-do with a precut bundle of 10" squares for a fast and fun finish.

Designed & Quilted by Jen Daly of Jen Daly Quilts

Skill Level
Beginner

Finished Sizes
Quilt Size: 61½" x 70½"
Block Size: 7½" x 7½"
Number of Blocks: 42

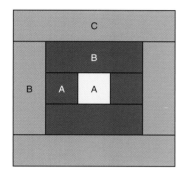

Framed Square
7½" x 7½" Finished Block
Make 42

Materials
- 42 (10") squares assorted prints*
- 1¼ yards cream print*
- ¾ yard multicolored floral*
- ⅝ yard blue print*
- 4¼ yards backing
- 70" x 78" batting
- Basic sewing tools and supplies

Fabrics from the Bee Vintage, Bee Cross Stitch and Bee Basics collections by Lori Holt for Riley Blake Designs used to make sample. EQ8 was used to design this quilt.

Project Notes
Read all instructions before beginning this project.

Stitch right sides together using a ¼" seam allowance unless otherwise specified.

Materials and cutting lists assume 40" of usable fabric width for yardage.

Arrows indicate directions to press seams.

WOF – width of fabric
HST – half-square triangle ◻
QST – quarter-square triangle ⊠

Cutting

From each assorted print square cut:

- 2 (2" x 8") C rectangles
- 4 (2" x 5") B rectangles
- 5 (2") A squares

From cream print cut:

- 97 (2" x 8") C rectangles

From multicolored floral cut:

- 7 (3½" x WOF) strips, stitch short ends to short ends, then subcut into:
  2 (3½" x 65") D and 2 (3½" x 62") E border strips

From blue print cut:

- 7 (2½" x WOF) binding strips

Here's a Tip

When choosing a background fabric, be sure that it provides enough contrast with your assorted prints. This is especially important if you have selected a precut bundle of 42 (10") squares because you'll be using all of them.

Completing the Blocks

1. Select one print A square, two A squares and two B rectangles of a second print, and two B rectangles and two C rectangles of a third print. Join the three A squares (Figure 1). Add B rectangles to the top and bottom.

2. Sew B rectangles of the third print to the sides (Figure 2). Sew C rectangles to the top and bottom to complete a Framed Square block.

3. Repeat steps 1 and 2 to make 42 blocks total.

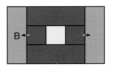

Figure 1

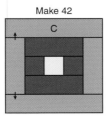

Make 42

Figure 2

Completing the Quilt

1. Referring to the Assembly Diagram, lay out seven block rows of seven cream C rectangles and six blocks each. Lay out eight sashing rows of seven assorted A squares and six cream C rectangles each. You will have 28 A squares left over.

2. Sew the sashing rows and the block rows. Join the rows to complete the quilt center. Press.

3. Sew the D and E border strips to the quilt top in alphabetical order.

4. Layer, baste, quilt as desired and bind referring to Quilting Basics. The photographed quilt was quilted with the Fast Flower pantograph by Munnich Design. ●

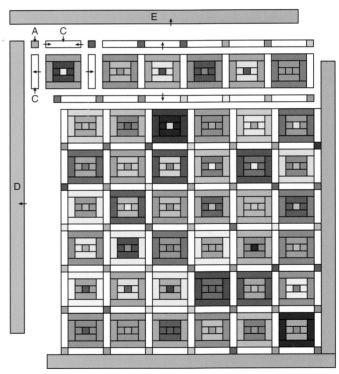

Square Dance
Assembly Diagram 61½" x 70½"

Inspiration

"I am expecting a new great-grandchild, so baby quilts and hearts are a perfect fit for the occasion!" —Bev Getschel

Slice of My Heart

Try this different take on a classic heart block—perfect for a new baby!

Designed & Quilted by Bev Getschel

Skill Level
Intermediate

Finished Sizes
Quilt Size: 46" x 46"
Block Size: 8" x 8"
Number of Blocks: 13

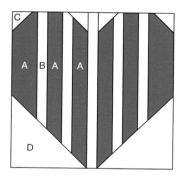

Sliced Heart
8" x 8" Finished Block
Make 13

Materials
- ⅓ yard each of 5 assorted red batiks*
- ¾ yard red batik stripe*
- 2½ yards white solid*
- 3¼ yards backing*
- 54" x 54" batting*
- Basic sewing tools and supplies

*Fabrics from Hoffman California-International Fabrics; Warm & Natural cotton batting from The Warm Company used to make sample. EQ8 was used to design this quilt.

Project Notes
Read all instructions before beginning this project.

Stitch right sides together using a ¼" seam allowance unless otherwise specified.

Materials and cutting lists assume 40" of usable fabric width for yardage.

Arrows indicate directions to press seams.

WOF – width of fabric
HST – half-square triangle ◺
QST – quarter-square triangle ⊠

Here's a Tip
Scant ¼" seam allowances are extra-important for this design.

Cutting

From each of 5 assorted red batiks cut:
- 2 (8½") A squares
- 2 (1½" x 22") K strips

From red batik stripe cut:
- 3 (8½") A squares
- 2 (1½" x 22") K strips
- 5 (2½" x WOF) binding strips

From white solid cut:
- 2 (15½") G squares, then cut twice diagonally ⊠
- 2 (6¾") H squares, then cut once diagonally ◺
- 26 (4¼") D squares
- 2 (2½" x 28½") F strips
- 4 (2½" x 22") M strips
- 10 (2½" x 8½") E strips
- 5 (1¾" x WOF) strips, stitch short ends to short ends, then subcut into:
  2 (1¾" x 42½") J and 2 (1¾" x 40") I border strips
- 52 (1½") C squares
- 12 (1" x 22") L strips
- 65 (1" x 8½") B strips

Completing the Blocks

1. Cut an A square into six pieces as shown (Figure 1).

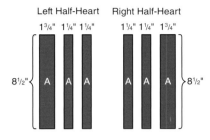

Figure 1

2. Sew B strips between the pieces of each half-heart (Figure 2).

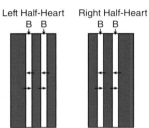

Figure 2

3. Refer to Sew & Flip Corners on page 12 and add two C and one D square to each half-heart, watching placement and orientation (Figure 3).

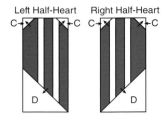

Figure 3

4. Join the left half-heart, a B strip and the right half-heart to complete a Heart block (Figure 4).

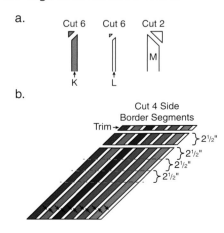

Figure 4

5. Repeat steps 1–4 to make 13 total blocks.

Completing the Border Strips

1. Cut the ends of six assorted K strips, six L strips and two M strips at right angles in the directions shown (Figure 5a). Set aside the M strips. Sew the K and L strips together, aligning the angled ends, to make the side strip set (Figure 5b). Trim one end at a 45-degree angle to the seams, and then cut four side border segments each 2½" wide.

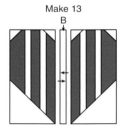

Figure 5

2. Similarly, cut the ends of six assorted K strips, six L strips and two M strips (Figure 6a). Set the M strips aside. Sew the K and L strips together, trim one end, and cut four top/bottom border segments each 2½" wide (Figure 6b).

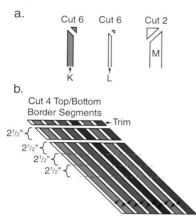

Figure 6

3. Join two side border segments and an M strip to make a side border strip (Figure 7). Make two. Join two top/bottom border segments and an M strip to make a top/bottom border strip. Make two.

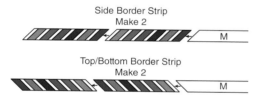

Figure 7

Completing the Quilt

1. Referring to the Assembly Diagram, lay out the blocks, E strips and F strips in five diagonal rows. Sew the rows.

2. Add G triangles to the ends of Rows 1, 2, 4 and 5. Join all five rows. Sew H triangles to the corners to complete the quilt center. Trim to 40" square, being sure to trim corners at 90-degree angles.

3. Sew the I and J border strips to the quilt top in alphabetical order.

4. Beginning at the top left of the quilt and starting ¼" from the corner, sew a side border strip to the left side; press open. Trim the end of the M strip even with the bottom of the quilt. In the same way, add a top/bottom border strip to the top of the quilt, press, and then trim M even. Sew a mitered seam between the side and top border strips.

5. Beginning at the bottom right corner of the quilt and starting ¼" from the corner, sew a side border strip to the right side. Trim the end of the M strip even with the top of the quilt. In the same way, add a top/bottom border strip to the bottom of the quilt, and then trim M even. Sew a mitered seam between the side and bottom border strips.

6. Layer, baste, quilt as desired and bind referring to Quilting Basics. The photographed quilt was quilted with diagonal lines. ●

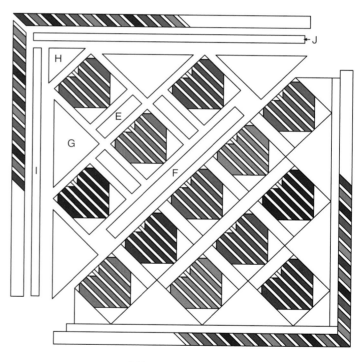

Slice of My Heart
Assembly Diagram 46" x 46"

Blueberry Cobbler

Grab your blue and green fat quarters and follow
this recipe for a quilt that cooks up quickly.

Design by Lyn Brown
Quilted by Cathy O'Brien

Skill Level
Beginner

Finished Sizes
Quilt Size: 45" x 62"
Block Size: 14" x 14"
Number of Blocks: 6

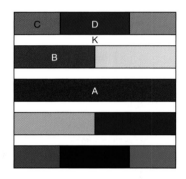

Block
14" x 14" Finished Block
Make 6

Materials
- 2½ yards background*
- 1 yard dark bright blue*
- 10 assorted blue and green fat quarters:*
    4 light to medium
    4 medium to dark
    2 dark
- 3 yards backing
- 53" x 70" batting
- Basic sewing tools and supplies

*Fabrics from the 885 Dot Batiks collection by Hoffman California-
International Fabrics. EQ8 was used to design this quilt.

Here's a Tip

While the sample keeps the placement of fabrics consistent throughout the blocks, Blueberry Cobbler would also be "tasty" using a heaping helping of spicy scraps.

Project Notes

Read all instructions before beginning this project.

Stitch right sides together using a ¼" seam allowance unless otherwise specified.

Materials and cutting lists assume 40" of usable fabric width for yardage and 20" for fat quarters.

Arrows indicate directions to press seams.

WOF – width of fabric
HST – half-square triangle ◻
QST – quarter-square triangle ⊠

Cutting

From background cut:
- 1 (48½" x WOF) strip, then subcut into:
    2 (5½" x 48½") G side border strips and
        2 (5½" x 41½") H top and bottom border strips
- 12 (1½" x WOF) strips, then subcut into:
    24 (1½" x 14½") K rectangles
- 4 (3½" x WOF) strips, then subcut into:
    3 (3½" x 14½") E rectangles and 2 (3½" x 31½")
        F rectangles

From dark bright blue cut:
- 3 (2½" x WOF) strips, then subcut into:
  6 (2½" x 14½") A rectangles and 4 (2½") J squares
- 6 (2½" x WOF) binding strips

From each light to medium fat quarter cut:
- 1 (7½" x 20") B strip

From each medium to dark fat quarter cut:
- 1 (4½" x 20") C strip

From each dark fat quarter cut:
- 1 (6½" x 20") D strip

From a variety of 10 fat quarters cut a total of:
- 34 (2½" x 6½") I rectangles

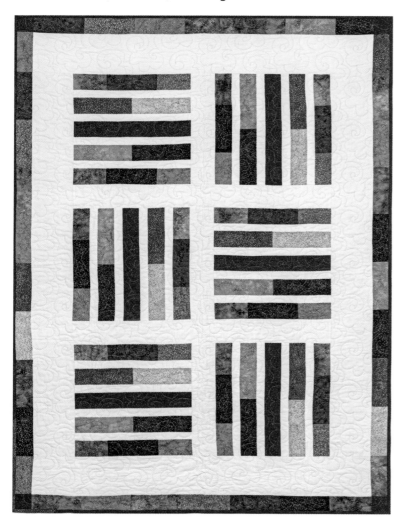

Here Are Tips

Press to the dark fabric as you go and press carefully to keep seams straight.

At each step check measurements for accuracy.

Completing the Blocks

Making the Rails

1. Rail 1 uses two different C rectangles, one D rectangle and a K rectangle. Sew a C rectangle to either side of the D rectangle along the long edge (Figure 1a). Cut into six Rail 1 pieces (Figure 1b). Pieces should measure 2½" x 14½". Then, add a K rectangle to the bottom long edge of each unit (Figure 1c). Rail 1 units should measure 2½" x 14½".

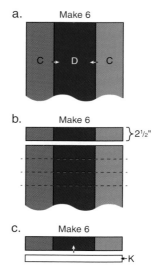

Figure 1

2. Rail 2 uses two different B rectangles. Sew the B rectangles together along a long edge (Figure 2a). Cut into six Rail 2 units (Figure 2b). Units should measure 2½" x 14½".

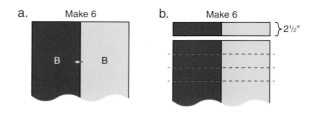

Figure 2

3. Rail 3 uses an A rectangle and two K rectangles. Sew a K rectangle to each side of the A rectangle along the long edge (Figure 3). Make six. Rail 3 units should measure 4½" x 14½".

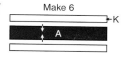

Make 6

Figure 3

4. Rail 4 uses two different B rectangles. Sew the B rectangles together along a long edge (Figure 4a). Cut into six Rail 4 units (Figure 4b). Rail 4 units should measure 2½" x 14½".

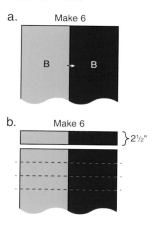

a. Make 6

b. Make 6 }2½"

Figure 4

5. Rail 5 uses two different C rectangles, one D rectangle and one K rectangle. Sew a C rectangle to either side of the D rectangle along the long edge (Figure 5a). Cut into six units (Figure 5b). Units should measure 2½" x 14½". Sew a K rectangle to the top of each unit (Figure 5c). Rail 5 units should measure 3½" x 14½".

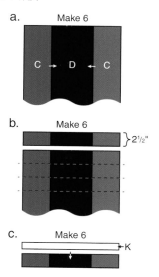

a. Make 6

b. Make 6 }2½"

c. Make 6 K

Figure 5

6. Sew a Rail 1 unit to the top of a Rail 2 unit (Figure 6a). Then, sew a Rail 4 unit to the top of a Rail 5 unit (Figure 6b). Units should measure 5½" x 14½". Make six of each.

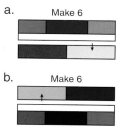

a. Make 6

b. Make 6

Figure 6

7. Sew a Rail 3 unit to the bottom of a Rail 1/Rail 2 unit from step 6 (Figure 7). Then, sew a Rail 4/Rail 5 unit from step 6 to the bottom to make a Blueberry block (Figure 7b). Unit should measure 14½" x 14½". Make six.

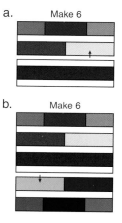

a. Make 6

b. Make 6

Figure 7

Making the Rows

1. Referring to the Assembly Diagram lay out the blocks in three rows of two blocks, noting orientation of the blocks. Then, sew an E rectangle between the two blocks in each row. Rows should measure 14½" x 31½".

2. Sew an F rectangle to the bottom of the first row and to the top of the third row.

Completing the Quilt

1. Referring to the Assembly Diagram, sew the rows together to make the quilt center. The unit should measure 31½" x 48½".

2. Sew the G border strips to the sides of the quilt center. Then, sew the H border strips to the top and bottom of the quilt center. The quilt should measure 41½" x 58½".

3. To make the pieced side borders, sew 10 I rectangles together along the short edges (Figure 8a). Measure the strip, then trim the strip evenly at both ends to make a 2½" x 58½" border. Make two.

a.

Side Border
Make 2

I →

b.

Top/Bottom Border
Make 2

J → I →

Figure 8

4. To make the pieced top and bottom borders, sew seven I rectangles together along the short edges. Measure the strip, then trim the strip evenly at both ends to make a 2½" x 41½" strip. Then, add a J square to either end (Figure 8b). The strip should measure 2½" x 45½". Make two.

5. Referring to the Assembly Diagram, sew the border strip from step 3 to the sides of the quilt center. Sew the border strip from step 4 to the top and bottom of the quilt center.

6. Layer, baste, quilt as desired and bind referring to Quilting Basics. The photographed quilt was quilted with a swirl design. ●

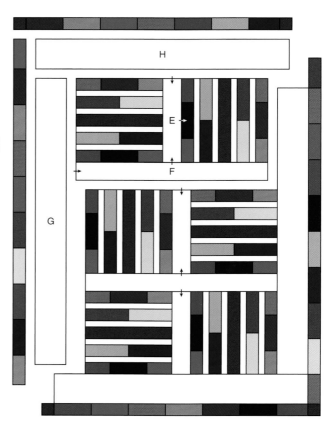

Blueberry Cobbler
Assembly Diagram 45" x 62"

Simply Charming

Bright 5" charm squares star in this fun and
unique table runner for all occasions.

Designed & Quilted by Julie Weaver

Skill Level
Confident Beginner

Finished Sizes
Runner Size: 19⅜" x 53¼"
Block Size: 4" x 4"
Number of Blocks: 23

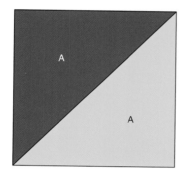

HST
4" x 4" Finished Block
Make 24

Materials
- 40 (5") squares assorted prints*
- ⅝ yard white solid
- ⅓ yard blue dot*
- 1⅞ yards backing
- 24" x 60" batting*
- Basic sewing tools and supplies

*Fabrics from the Sweet Melodies collection by American Jane for Moda
Fabrics; Warm & Natural cotton batting from The Warm Company used
to make sample.

Project Notes
Read all instructions before beginning this project.

Stitch right sides together using a ¼" seam
allowance unless otherwise specified.

Materials and cutting lists assume 40" of usable
fabric width for yardage.

Arrows indicate directions to press seams.

WOF – width of fabric
HST – half-square triangle ◲
QST – quarter-square triangle ◱

Cutting

From each of 16 assorted print (5") squares cut:
- 4 (2½") F squares (64 total);
  the remaining 24 (5") squares are A squares

From white solid cut:
- 4 (7") B squares, then cut twice diagonally ◱
- 2 (4") C squares, then cut once diagonally ◲
- 7 (1½" x WOF) D/E/G/H border strips

From blue dot cut:
- 4 (2½" x WOF) binding strips

Here's a Tip

*I made the HST units using 5" squares and then
trimmed them to 4½". This makes for easier
sewing and more accurate results.*

Completing the Blocks

1. Refer to Half-Square Triangles and use the A squares to make 24 HST blocks (Figure 1). Trim each to 4½" square, centering the diagonal seams.

Make and Trim 24

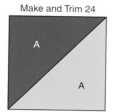

Figure 1

Completing the Runner

1. Referring to the Assembly Diagram, lay out the blocks and B triangles in nine diagonal rows, watching block rotation. You will have one block left over. Sew the blocks into rows and join the rows. Sew C triangles to the corners to complete the runner center. Press well.

2. Trim edges ¼" outside the outer seam intersections, being sure to trim corners at 90-degree angles.

3. Sew the D/E/G/H border strips together, short ends to short ends. Referring to Determining Border Lengths on page 8, measure and cut D and E border strips and sew borders to the quilt center.

4. Stitch two sets of 23 F squares together, adjusting seams as necessary to fit the long sides of the runner. Stitch one set to each long side. Stitch two sets of nine F squares together, adjusting seams to fit the short sides of the runner. Stitch one set to each short side.

5. Again referring to Determining Border Lengths, measure and cut G and H border strips from the white pieced border strip and sew borders to the quilt center.

6. Layer, baste, quilt as desired and bind referring to Quilting Basics. The photographed quilt was quilted with an edge-to-edge loop and meander design. ●

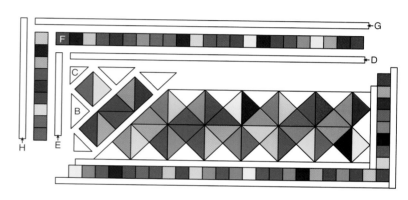

Simply Charming
Assembly Diagram 19⅜" x 53¼"

HALF-SQUARE TRIANGLES

Half-square triangles (HSTs) are a basic unit of quilting used in many blocks or on their own. This construction method will yield two HSTs.

1. Refer to the pattern for size to cut squares. The standard formula is to add ⅞" to the finished size of the square. Cut two squares from different colors this size. For example, for a 3" finished HST unit, cut 3⅞" squares.

2. Draw a diagonal line from corner to corner on the wrong side of the lightest color square. Layer the squares right sides together. Stitch ¼" on either side of the drawn line (Figure A).

Figure A

3. Cut the squares apart on the drawn line, leaving a ¼" seam allowance and making two HST units referring to Figure B.

Figure B

4. Open the HST units and press seam allowances toward the darker fabric making two HST units (Figure C). ●

Figure C

Batik Waffles

Precut 2½" x WOF strips make this quilt quick and fun to piece. It's perfect for a group project since minor variations in piecing are not problematic.

Designed & Quilted by Carol Wilhoit of CarolQuilts

Skill Level
Beginner

Finished Sizes
Quilt size: 42" x 56"
Block size: 14" x 14"
Number of blocks: 12

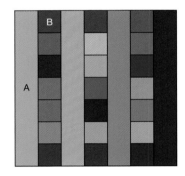

Waffle
14" x 14" Finished Block
Make 12

Materials
- 40 precut (2½" x WOF) strips assorted batiks
- ½ yard binding fabric
- 3 yards backing
- 52" x 66" batting
- Thread
- Basic sewing tools and supplies

Project Notes
Read all instructions before beginning this project.

Stitch right sides together using a ¼" seam allowance unless otherwise specified.

Materials and cutting lists assume 40" of usable fabric width.

Arrows indicate directions to press seams.

WOF – width of fabric
HST – half-square triangle ◻
QST – quarter-square triangle ⊠

Cutting

Here's a Tip
Some batiks have definite right and wrong sides, but it's not always easy to tell them apart. When cutting, make a mark in the seam allowance on the wrong side so that all of the units share the same right side when sewn together.

From precut batik strips cut:
- 48 total (2½" x 14½") A strips
- 63 total (2½" x 11") B strips

From binding fabric cut:
- 6 (2½" x WOF) binding strips

Inspiration

"I was eager to make this design with batik fabrics that are similar in color and value to see how they visually blend together. The quilt is so quickly pieced that it is easy and fun to try variations. Each one looks so different!" —Carol Wilhoit

Completing the Blocks

1. To make a strip set, lay out seven different B strips in a pleasing arrangement; stitch together lengthwise. Make nine strip sets. Cut 36 (2½" x 14½") pieced B units from strip sets (Figure 1).

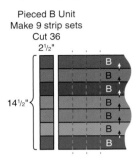

Pieced B Unit
Make 9 strip sets
Cut 36
2½"
14½"

Figure 1

2. Arrange four different A strips and three different pieced B units as shown (Figure 2); sew together to complete one Waffle block. Make 12.

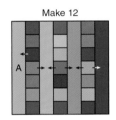

Make 12

Figure 2

Here's a Tip

When sewing the block together, place the pieced strip on top to keep the pressed seam allowances from flipping to the wrong direction. Also, pin the strips together at the midpoint and end to keep the strips aligned and prevent the pieced strip from stretching.

Completing the Quilt

1. Referring to the Assembly Diagram and noting block orientation, arrange the blocks in four rows. Sew the blocks into rows then sew the rows together to complete the quilt top.

2. Stitch around the perimeter of the quilt top, close to the edge, to secure the seams.

3. Layer, baste, quilt as desired and bind referring to Quilting Basics. The photographed quilt was quilted with a circular spiral design. ●

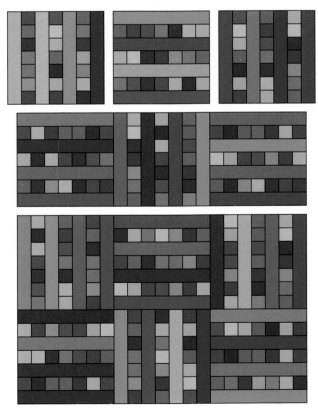

Batik Waffles
Assembly Diagram 42" x 56"

Stairway to Heaven

A simple rail fence pattern can be enhanced by using a carefully selected gradation of fabrics. Use the seams as a quilting guide to ensure a hassle-free quilt in a short time.

Designed & Quilted by Preeti Harris of Sew Preeti Quilts

Skill Level
Beginner

Finished Sizes
Quilt Size: 60" x 80"
Block Size: 10" x 10"
Number of Blocks: 48

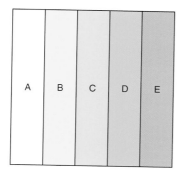

Yellow
10" x 10" Finished Block
Make 24

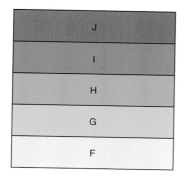

Orange
10" x 10" Finished Block
Make 24

Materials
- 1½ yards white solid*
- ⅔ yard each very light yellow, light yellow, medium yellow, dark yellow, very light orange, light orange, medium orange, dark/reddish orange and very dark reddish orange batiks*
- 5 yards backing*
- 68" x 88" batting
- Basic sewing tools and supplies

Fabrics from Island Batik used to make sample. EQ8 was used to design this quilt.

Project Notes
Read all instructions before beginning this project.

Stitch right sides together using a ¼" seam allowance unless otherwise specified.

Materials and cutting lists assume 40" of usable fabric width for yardage.

Arrows indicate directions to press seams.

WOF – width of fabric
HST – half-square triangle ◻
QST – quarter-square triangle ⊠

Cutting

From white solid cut:
- 8 (2½" x WOF) A strips
- 8 (2½" x WOF) binding strips

From very light yellow batik cut:
- 8 (2½" x WOF) B strips

From light yellow batik cut:
- 8 (2½" x WOF) C strips

From medium yellow batik cut:
- 8 (2½" x WOF) D strips

From dark yellow batik cut:
- 8 (2½" x WOF) E strips

From very light orange batik cut:
- 8 (2½" x WOF) F strips

From light orange batik cut:
- 8 (2½" x WOF) G strips

From medium orange batik cut:
- 8 (2½" x WOF) H strips

From dark/reddish orange batik cut:
- 8 (2½" x WOF) I strips

From very dark reddish orange batik cut:
- 8 (2½" x WOF) J strips

Completing the Blocks

Yellow Blocks

1. Sew one each of the A, B, C, D and E strips together along long edges to make one strip set A (Figure 1). Make eight.

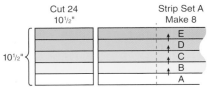

Figure 1

2. Cut each strip set into three 10½" Yellow blocks. Cut 24 total Yellow blocks.

Orange Blocks

1. Sew one each of the F, G, H, I and J strips together along long edges to make one strip set B (Figure 2). Make eight.

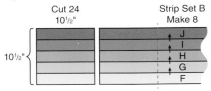

Figure 2

2. Cut each strip set into three 10½" Orange blocks. Cut 24 total Orange blocks.

Completing the Quilt

1. Referring to the Assembly Diagram, arrange and sew together the yellow and orange blocks, alternating, in eight rows of six blocks.

2. Join the rows to complete the quilt top.

3. Layer, baste, quilt as desired and bind referring to Quilting Basics. The photographed quilt was quilted with a serpentine stitch in a 2" grid. ●

Stairway to Heaven
Assembly Diagram 60" x 80"

Crisscross Throw

Create a trellis-like pattern by inserting a white strip in the center of each 5" charm square. A pretty floral collection is a good choice for this design.

Designed & Quilted by Chris Malone

Skill Level
Confident Beginner

Finished Sizes
Quilt Size: 54" x 54"
Block Size: 4½" x 4½"
Number of Blocks: 144

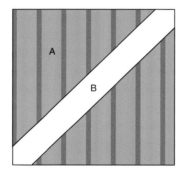

Crisscross
4½" x 4½" Finished Block
Make 144

Materials
- 144 precut 5" A squares in assorted aqua, rose, yellow, black tonals and prints
- 1¼ yards white solid
- ½ yard black with white dots
- Backing to size
- Batting to size
- Square ruler at least 5" x 5" (optional)
- Basic sewing tools and supplies

Project Notes
Read all instructions before beginning this project.

Stitch right sides together using a ¼" seam allowance unless otherwise specified.

Materials and cutting lists assume 40" of usable fabric width for yardage.

WOF – width of fabric
HST – half-square triangle ◺
QST – quarter-square triangle ⊠

Cutting

From white solid cut:
- 5 (7½" x WOF) strips, then subcut into: 144 (1¼" x 7½") B strips

From black with white dots cut:
- 6 (2¼" x WOF) binding strips

Completing the Quilt
1. Cut each A square in half diagonally, from corner to corner, keeping the triangle pairs together.

2. Fold an A triangle in half and finger-press a crease at the midpoint of the cut edge. Repeat with matching A triangle. Fold a B strip in half lengthwise and finger-press a crease.

3. Matching center creases, pin B to A triangle and stitch as shown in Figure 1. Repeat with remaining A, sewing it to the opposite side of B.

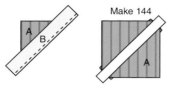

Make 144

Figure 1

4. Repeat steps 2 and 3 using all the triangle pairs and white strips to make 144 blocks.

5. Randomly divide blocks into two groups of 72 blocks. Press one set of blocks with seam allowances toward A and the other set of blocks with seam allowances toward B so that seams will nest when joining the blocks.

6. Trim each block to 5" x 5" with the white strip centered diagonally. If using a square ruler for trimming, align the diagonal line down the center of the strip.

7. Referring to the Assembly Diagram, arrange the blocks into 12 rows of 12 blocks each, alternating the direction of the seam allowances and the B strips so a trellis design is formed with the white strips.

8. Sew the blocks together in each row.

9. Sew the rows together to complete the quilt top.

10. Layer, quilt as desired and bind referring to Quilting Basics. ●

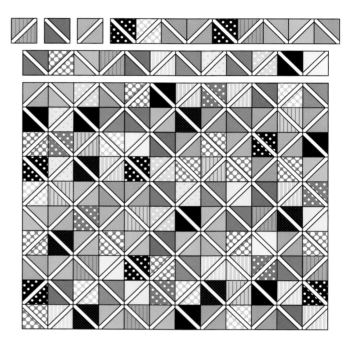

Crisscross Throw
Assembly Diagram 54" x 54"

Sidestep

By using square-in-a-square units and careful fabric placement,
you can make this gorgeous quilt with fat quarters.

Design by Nancy Scott
Quilted by Masterpiece Quilting

Skill Level
Confident Beginner

Finished Size
Quilt Size: 58½" x 72"

Materials
- 17 fat quarters assorted prints and tonals
- ⅔ yard dark blue tonal
- ⅞ yard gray tonal
- Backing to size
- Batting to size
- Thread
- Basic sewing tools and supplies

Project Notes
Read all instructions before beginning this project.

Stitch right sides together using a ¼" seam allowance unless otherwise specified.

Materials and cutting lists assume 40" of usable fabric width for yardage and 20" for fat quarters.

WOF – width of fabric

Cutting

From assorted fat quarters:
- Cut 4 (5" x 9½") A rectangles from each fat quarter.
- Cut a total of 10 (5") B squares.
- Cut 8 (3⅛") squares from each fat quarter and 1 (3⅛") square to match each B square.
    Cut each square in half on 1 diagonal to make 292 D triangles.

Note: There are extra A rectangles (64 needed) and D triangles (280 needed) to help with color placement.

From dark blue tonal:
- Cut 7 (2¾" x WOF) binding strips.

Note: See Here's a Tip on page 39 for more binding information.

From gray tonal:
- Cut 7 (3⅝" x WOF) strips.
    Subcut strips into 70 (3⅝") C squares.

Here's a Tip

The binding was cut wider than usual to act as a narrow border/binding. Cut the excess batting and backing ¼" beyond the edge of the quilt top after quilting to allow the excess binding width to be filled with batting and backing when the quilt is finished. Align with the edge of the quilt top and stitch ¼" from the edge of the quilt top as usual.

Completing the Quilt

Press all seams open to reduce bulk.

1. Referring to the Assembly Diagram, arrange the pieces for the top four rows on a flat surface, matching the D triangles to the A rectangles or B squares as needed to create the pattern and to avoid the same fabrics touching in adjacent rows.

2. From arrangement, select one C square and two sets of two matching D triangles from the top row.

3. Sew two matching D triangles to two adjacent sides of C as shown in Figure 1; press.

C-D Unit

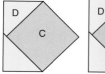

Figure 1

4. Sew a second set of matching D squares to the remaining sides of C to complete one C-D unit, again referring to Figure 1. Place back in the arranged top row.

5. Repeat steps 2–4 to complete the remaining C-D units in the row.

6. Join the C-D units with the A rectangles to complete the top row; press.

7. Continue to make C-D units and join with A rect-angles and B squares to complete the remaining arranged rows.

8. Join the completed rows; press. Set aside.

9. Repeat steps 1–8 to arrange and complete the remaining rows.

10. Join the row sections to complete the quilt top; press.

11. Create a quilt sandwich referring to Quilting Basics.

12. Layer and quilt as desired. Bind the quilt referring to Here's a Tip and Quilting Basics. ●

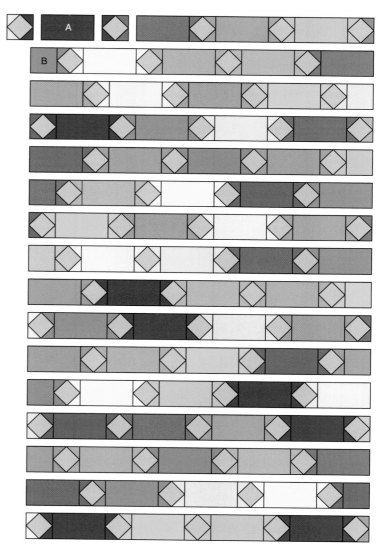

Sidestep
Assembly Diagram 58½" x 72"

Summer Breeze

A fun collection of batiks makes this a stunning quilt.

Design by Lyn Brown
Quilted by Cathy O'Brien

Skill Level
Confident Beginner

Finished Sizes
Quilt Size: 68" x 88"
Block Size: 18" x 18" finished
Number of Blocks: 12

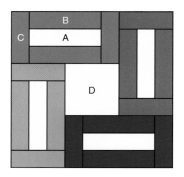

Breeze 1
18" x 18" Finished Block
Make 6

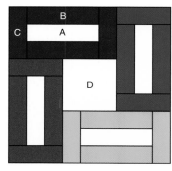

Breeze 2
18" x 18" Finished Block
Make 6

Materials
- ⅝ yard each red, burgundy, purple, orange and gold batiks
- ⅝ yard each 2 different green print batiks
- 1⅓ yards blue batik
- 3⅓ yards cream batik
- Backing to size
- Batting to size
- Thread
- Basic sewing tools and supplies

Project Notes
Read all instructions before beginning this project.

Stitch right sides together using a ¼" seam allowance unless otherwise specified.

Materials and cutting lists assume 40" of usable fabric width for yardage.

WOF – width of fabric

Cutting

From red, burgundy, purple, orange & gold batiks:
- Cut 1 (8½" x WOF) strip each fabric.
  Subcut strip into 12 (2½" x 8½") B strips each fabric.
- Cut 1 (6½" x WOF) strip each fabric.
  Subcut strip into 12 (2½" x 6½") C strips each fabric.

From green print batiks:
- Cut 1 (8½" x WOF) strip each fabric.
  Subcut strip into 12 (2½" x 8½") B strips each fabric.
- Cut 1 (6½" x WOF) strip each fabric.
  Subcut strip into 12 (2½" x 6½") C strips each fabric.

From blue batik:
- Cut 1 (8½" x WOF) strip.
  Subcut strip into 12 (2½" x 8½") B strips.
- Cut 1 (6½" x WOF) strip.
  Subcut strip into 12 (2½" x 6½") C strips.
- Cut 9 (2¼" x WOF) binding strips.

From cream batik:

- Cut 3 (8½" x WOF) strips.
  Subcut strips into 48 (2½" x 8½") A strips.
- Cut 2 (6½" x WOF) strips.
  Subcut strips into 12 (6½") D squares.
- Cut 4 (2½" x WOF) strips.
  Subcut strips into 8 (2½" x 18½") E strips.
- Cut 5 (2½" x WOF) F strips.
- Cut 8 (5½" x WOF) G/H strips.

Completing the Blocks

1. Select one A strip and two each same-fabric B and C strips.

2. Sew the A strip between two B strips as shown in Figure 1; press.

3. Add C strips to opposite ends of the A-B unit to complete one A-B-C unit as shown in Figure 2.

4. Repeat steps 1–3 to make a total of 48 A-B-C units (six each of the eight fabrics).

Figure 1

A-B-C Unit
Make 48

Figure 2

PARTIAL SEAMS

Use partial seaming to join a variety of unevenly placed pieces in a block or unevenly placed blocks or sections in a quilt.

1. Lay out the block pieces or quilt sections around the center piece or block as shown in Figure A.

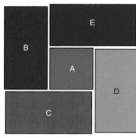

Figure A

2. Referring to Figure B, stitch A (center square) to B (first section) beginning approximately 2" from the bottom corner of A. Finger-press A away from B.

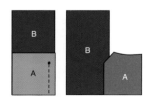

Figure B

3. Working counterclockwise, join C (second section) to the A-B unit as shown in Figure C, stitching the entire length of the seam. Press seam toward C.

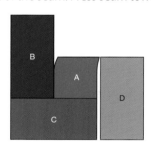

Figure C

4. Match and join D (third section) to A-C edge referring again to Figure C, completing the entire length of the seam. Press seam toward D.

5. Join E (fourth section) to the A-D edge, again completing the entire length of the seam, as shown in Figure D. Be sure to keep B (first section) out of the way when stitching.

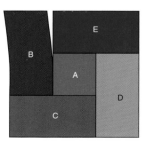

Figure D

6. Complete the assembly by finishing the A-B seam that was partially sewn in step 2. Fold over C and match the B edge to the A-E edge. Lower the machine needle at the end of the A-B seam, backstitch to secure and complete the A-B seam as shown in red in Figure E. Press seam toward B, completing the block or quilt section (Figure F). ●

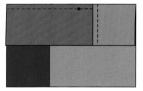

Figure E

Figure F

5. Select one each red, orange, green 1 and green 2 A-B-C unit and one D square.

6. Sew one A-B-C unit to D with a partial seam referring to Partial Seams.

7. Add a second A-B-C unit to D on the longest side of the stitched unit as shown in Figure 3; press.

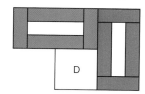

Figure 3

8. Add a third and fourth A-B-C unit to D as in step 7; press.

9. Complete the stitching on the partial seam to complete one Breeze 1 block; press.

10. Repeat steps 5–9 with the remaining same-fabric A-B-C units, adding the units to D in the same color order, to complete a total of six Breeze 1 blocks.

11. Repeat steps 5–9 with the remaining A-B-C units to complete a total of six Breeze 2 blocks referring to the block diagram for color order.

Completing the Quilt
Refer to the Assembly Diagram as necessary for quilt assembly.

1. Select and join one Breeze 2 and two Breeze 1 blocks with two E strips to make an X row; press. Repeat to make a second X row.

2. Select and join one Breeze 1 block and two Breeze 2 blocks with two E strips to make a Y row; press. Repeat to make a second Y row.

3. Join the F strips on the short ends to make one long strip; press. Subcut strip into three 2½" x 58½" F strips.

4. Arrange and join the X and Y rows with the F strips to complete the pieced center; press.

5. Join the G/H strips on the short ends to make one long strip; press. Subcut strip into two each 5½" x 78½" G strips and 5½" x 68½" H strips.

6. Sew G strips to opposite long sides and H strips to the top and bottom of the pieced center to complete the quilt top; press.

7. Create a quilt sandwich referring to Quilting Basics.

8. Quilt as desired.

9. Bind edges referring to Quilting Basics to finish. ●

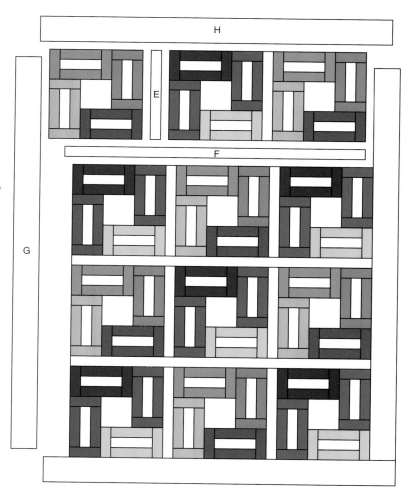

Summer Breeze
Assembly Diagram 68" x 88"

Wash Day

This super-simple quilt, reminiscent of long-ago visits to Grandma's house, could be just the pattern you're looking for.

Design by Tricia Lynn Maloney
Quilted by Karen Shields of Karen's Quilting Studio

Skill Level
Beginner

Finished Sizes
Quilt Size: 53" x 68"
Block Size: 9" x 12"
Number of Blocks: 13

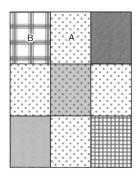

Elongated Nine-Patch
9" x 12" Finished Block
Make 13

Materials
- 10–12 fat quarters assorted red, gray and blue prints and plaids
- ⅝ yard blue print
- ⅞ yard red solid
- 1 yard white-with-blue dot
- Backing to size
- Batting to size
- Thread
- Basic sewing tools and supplies

Project Notes
Read all instructions before beginning this project.

Stitch right sides together using a ¼" seam allowance unless otherwise specified.

Materials and cutting lists assume 40" of usable fabric width for yardage and 20" for fat quarters.

WOF – width of fabric

Cutting

From assorted red, gray & blue prints & plaids:
- Cut 10 (9½" x 12½") C rectangles.
- Cut 65 (3½" x 4½") B rectangles.

From blue print:
- Cut 7 (2¼" x WOF) binding strips.

From red solid:
- Cut 6 (4½" x WOF) D/E strips.

From white-with-blue dot:
- Cut 1 (9½" x WOF) strip.
   Subcut strip into 2 (9½" x 12½") C rectangles and 12 (3½" x 4½") A rectangles.
- Cut 4 (4½" x WOF) strips.
   Subcut strips into 40 (3½" x 4½") A rectangles to total 52 A rectangles.

Completing the Blocks
1. Referring to the block diagram, arrange and sew four A and five B rectangles into three rows; press. Sew rows together to complete one Elongated Nine-Patch block; press. Repeat to make a total of 13 Elongated Nine-Patch blocks.

Completing the Quilt

1. Arrange and join three Elongated Nine-Patch blocks and two C squares to make a 3-block row as shown in Figure 1; press. Repeat to make a total of three 3-block rows.

3-Block Row
Make 3

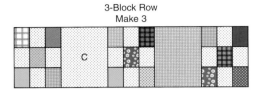

Figure 1

2. Referring to Figure 2, arrange and join two Elongated Nine-Patch blocks and three C rectangles to make a 2-block row; press. Repeat to make a second 2-block row.

2-Block Row
Make 2

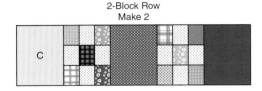

Figure 2

3. Alternately sew 3-block and 2-block rows together to complete the quilt center; press.

4. Sew D/ E strips together on the short ends to make one long strip; press. Subcut strip into two each 4½" x 60½" D and 4½" x 53½" E strips.

5. Sew D strips to the opposite sides of the quilt center and E strips to the top and bottom to complete the quilt top; press.

6. Create a quilt sandwich referring to Quilting Basics.

7. Quilt as desired. The sample quilt was machine-quilted with a four-petal motif.

8. Join the binding strips and bind the edges referring to Quilting Basics. ●

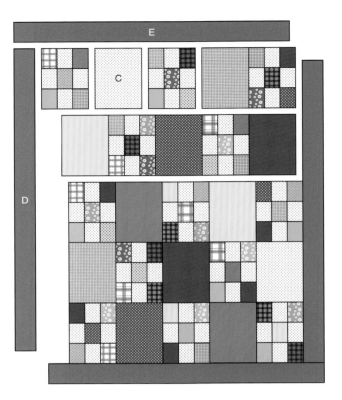

Wash Day
Assembly Diagram 53" x 68"

Quilting Basics

The following is a reference guide. For more information, consult a comprehensive quilting book.

Quilt Backing & Batting

Cut your backing and batting 8" larger than the finished quilt-top size and 4" larger for quilts smaller than 50" square. *Note: Check with longarm quilter about their requirements, if applicable. For baby quilts not going to a longarm quilter 4"–6" overall may be sufficient.* If preparing the backing from standard-width fabrics, remove the selvages and sew two or three lengths together; press seams open. If using 108"-wide fabric, trim to size on the straight grain of the fabric. Prepare batting the same size as your backing.

Quilting

1. Press quilt top on both sides and trim all loose threads. *Note: If you are sending your quilt to a longarm quilter, contact them for specifics about preparing your quilt for quilting.*
2. Mark quilting design on quilt top. Make a quilt sandwich by layering the backing right side down, batting and quilt top centered right side up on flat surface and smooth out. Baste layers together using pins, thread basting or spray basting to hold. *Note: Tape or pin backing to surface to hold taut while layering and avoid puckers.*
3. Quilt as desired by hand or machine. Remove pins or basting as you quilt.
4. Trim batting and backing edges even with raw edges of quilt top.

Binding the Quilt

1. Join binding strips on short ends with diagonal seams to make one long strip; trim seams to ¼" and press seams open (Figure 1).

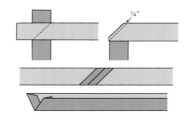

Figure 1

2. Fold ½" of one short end to wrong side and press. Fold the binding strip in half with wrong sides together along length, again referring to Figure 1; press.
3. Starting about 3" from the folded short end, sew binding to quilt top edges, matching raw edges and using a ¼" seam. Stop stitching ¼" from corner and backstitch (Figure 2).

Figure 2

4. Fold binding up at a 45-degree angle to seam and then down even with quilt edges, forming a pleat at corner (Figure 3).

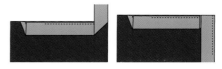

Figure 3

5. Resume stitching from corner edge as shown in Figure 3, down quilt side, backstitching ¼" from next corner. Repeat, mitering all corners, stitching to within 3" of starting point.
6. Trim binding, leaving enough length to tuck inside starting end and complete stitching (Figure 4).

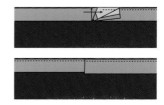

Figure 4

7. If stitching binding by hand, machine-sew binding to the front of the quilt and fold to the back before stitching. If stitching by machine, machine-sew binding to back of the quilt and fold to the front before stitching.

Special Thanks

Please join us in thanking the talented designers whose work is featured in this collection.

Lyn Brown
Blueberry Cobbler, 20
Summer Breeze, 40

Jen Daly
Square Dance, 13

Scott A. Flanagan
Sandy Shores, 6

Bev Getschel
Slice of My Heart, 17

Preeti Harris
Stairway to Heaven, 31

Andy Knowlton
Wish Making, 3

Chris Malone
Crisscross Throw, 34

Tricia Lynn Maloney
Wash Day, 44

Nancy Scott
Sidestep, 37

Wendy Sheppard
Color Me Happy, 11

Julie Weaver
Simply Charming, 25

Carol Wilhoit
Batik Waffles, 28

Supplies

We would like to thank the following manufacturers who provided materials to make sample projects for this book.

Wish Making, page 3: Fabrics from Berry Basket by April Rosenthal for Moda Fabrics.

Sandy Shores, page 6: Warm & Natural: Warm 100 batting from The Warm Company.

Color Me Happy, page 11: Fabrics from Bella Solids by Moda Fabrics; 50 wt. Mako thread from Aurifil; Tuscany silk batting from Hobbs Bonded Fibers.

Square Dance, page 13: Fabrics from the Bee Vintage, Bee Cross Stitch and Bee Basics collections by Lori Holt for Riley Blake Designs.

Slice of My Heart, page 17: Fabrics from Hoffman California-International Fabrics; Warm & Natural cotton batting from The Warm Company.

Blueberry Cobbler, page 20: Fabrics from the 885 Dot Batiks collection by Hoffman California-International Fabrics.

Simply Charming, page 25: Fabrics from the Sweet Melodies collection by American Jane for Moda Fabrics; Warm & Natural cotton batting from The Warm Company.

Stairway to Heaven, page 31: Fabrics from Island Batik.

 Published by Annie's, 306 East Parr Road, Berne, IN 46711. Printed in USA. Copyright © 2023, 2024 Annie's. All rights reserved. This publication may not be reproduced in part or in whole without written permission from the publisher.

RETAIL STORES: If you would like to carry this publication or any other Annie's publications, visit AnniesWSL.com.

Every effort has been made to ensure that the instructions in this publication are complete and accurate. We cannot, however, take responsibility for human error, typographical mistakes or variations in individual work. Please visit AnniesCustomerService.com to check for pattern updates.

ISBN: 978-1-64025-637-8

3 4 5 6 7 8 9